The Secret of Toddler Sharing

Why Sharing Is Hard and How to Make It Easier

by Elizabeth Crary, M.S.

Parenting Press

Seattle | Washington

Contents

All rights reserved
ISBN 978-1-936903-08-5
www.ParentingPress.com | 800.992.6657

The Secret of
Toddler Sharing

The secret of toddler sharing is — *toddlers don't share*. Truly. They don't have the concept. They don't have the skills. They don't have the necessary delayed gratification.

But, you say, "I have seen toddlers share." Yes, I have too. These few young kids are the exception — either their temperament is flexible and yielding, they are very sensitive to others' feelings, or they were simply born with a generous, giving nature. True sharing rarely happens before three years of age. However, sharing is an excellent *goal* to work actively towards during toddlerhood — just not a reasonable expectation.

❊ Can Toddlers Learn to Share?

Fortunately, there are several things you can do to hasten your toddler's ability to share and get along peacefully with others. We will look at the nature of sharing, factors affecting sharing, and some specific things you can do to encourage sharing.

....

Challenge 1: *Toddlers are just* beginning *to learn self-restraint and social skills.*

....

When toddlers turn to you as they reach to pull the cat's tail or touch a forbidden object, they are not saying, "Ha, ha, ha. Catch me if you can," the way it often feels. Instead, they are usually saying, "Help me! I know I'm not supposed to do this, but I can't stop myself. The temptation is too great." Their situation is similar to a chocoholic trying to lose weight who sees a luscious piece of chocolate cake at a social gathering, and turns to a friend and says, "Get me away from here. The temptation is immense." Without self-restraint children cannot defer their wishes when asked to wait for a toy or turn or attention.

This lack of self-restraint prompts much of their unwanted action — running away in the parking lot, pulling the heads off the daffodils, walking through water puddles, and throwing, hitting, or biting when frustrated or angry.

Possible solution: Approach sharing as a skill to be learned, rather than an act of will or a product of maturation. If you teach specific skills and strategies, you can speed up the learning process. If you don't teach needed skills, your children may pick up some of the skills — or they may not.

The meaning of sharing

There is a fundamental difference in how adults and toddlers think about sharing. Life with toddlers is easier when you understand their point of view.

Adults' view: Kids play "nicely" together. Both (all) kids play peacefully — they divide toys, wait for a turn, and use the toys respectfully — no grabbing, pushing, whining, yelling, etc.

Toddlers' view: Adults expect them to give ownership of "their toys" to other children — pleasantly! Toddlers don't understand the difference between sharing a toy and giving it up permanently. So toddlers often become afraid the other child will not return their toy, and they act on that fear by having a tantrum, hitting, pushing, yelling, or behaving obnoxiously until the toy is returned. (See Challenge 2.)

From a practical point of view, sharing with toddlers has two aspects — (1) *taking turns* (Ava rides the truck around the room and then lets Molly ride it around) and (2) *dividing items* (Mark splits his hunk of play dough (or crackers) and gives half to Carlos).

Concepts in sharing

There are five concepts children need in learning to share:

- Mine
- Not mine
- Not mine have owners
- I can own it while you use it
- Joint ownership

You can tell what level your toddler is on by listening to his or her language. *Mine* is an important first step (however frustrating) because a person cannot truly share if they do not own anything. *Not mine* and *Not mine have owners* are important in learning to respect boundaries. The concept of *I can own it while you use it* is necessary for toddlers to let others use their things without fear of loss. *Joint ownership*, that two or more people can own something, is beyond most toddlers.

You will have to help your toddler learn these concepts.

....

Challenge 2: *Toddlers have an immature understanding of ownership.*

....

Toddlers believe that if they have an item, it belongs to them. Correspondingly, if the item is in your hands, it belongs to you. With toddlers, possession is not 9/10th of the law, it is 100% of the law. If they have it, they own it. It is totally theirs. Therefore, toddlers are very reluctant to let another use it, even for a moment, because it will not belong to them anymore. However, this belief does not prevent them from trying to take an item that they want from someone else.

Possible solution: Teach kids to take turns so that they learn that they can own a thing while another person uses it. However, before we consider specific sharing strategies, let's look at some factors that influence sharing. (See "Taking turns" in the section "Five Sharing Strategies.")

✳ Factors Affecting Sharing

There are three factors that affect how easily a child learns to share: developmental stage, temperament, and personal experience.

Developmental stage

A child's developmental stage influences sharing, and each child has his own developmental timetable. One major developmental task for toddlers is to learn to be independent. Further, toddlers are very concerned with their own needs and wishes. As a result, toddlers want to do things for themselves, have their own ideas about how things should happen, and say "No" many times each day.

This focus on independence, their lack of relf-restraint, and their ignorance about ownership contributes to toddlers' inability to share. (See *Is This a Phase? Child Development & Parent Strategies, Birth to 6 Years* by Helen F. Neville.)

Temperament

Another factor that affects sharing is a child''s temperament. There are ten temperament traits (see sidebar). Each temperament trait is helpful in some situations and difficult in others. Of these ten traits, five directly influence a child''s ability to share. (See *Temperament Tools* by Helen F. Neville and Diane Clark Johnson.)

Ten temperament traits

Activity
Adaptability
Approach
Distractibility
Emotional sensitivity
Intensity
Mood
Persistence
Regularity
Sensory awareness

Persistence. If a child is very persistent, he or she will continue to try to get a wanted toy. If the child with the toy holds on, persistent children may pull harder or try several strategies to get the toy. Children with low persistence generally give up if they meet resistance.

Intensity. Some children are more intense than others. These kids with high intensity cry louder, run harder, and generally put more energy into everything they do. If another child tries to take a toy they are using, these kids often react with an ear-piercing cry or a hard shove. Conversely, toddlers with low intensity may not be done using a toy, but rarely say anything if it is taken away from them.

Emotional sensitivity. Some children are very aware of their feelings and/or those of other people. Other children are unaware of their own feelings and oblivious to those of other children or adults. Although you can teach these kids to recognize and name feelings it can take a great deal of effort. It is usually easier for kids who are sensitive to others' emotions to learn to share.

Flexibility. Children who are highly adaptable find it comparatively easy to share. They can change activities and do (or use) something else. On the other hand, children with low flexibility, — sometimes called natural planners, get an idea in their mind and have a hard time changing direction. These children often have difficulty with sharing and with transitions. If you can help them create a new plan, things often work better.

Approach. Some children are naturally more curious, others naturally more cautious. Toddlers who are intensely curious may have difficulty waiting for a turn and try to take toys from other kids.

Experience

A child's experience with other people's sharing influences how early and easily she learns to share herself.

Family modeling. Parents and caregivers can encourage the process of sharing by deliberately sharing with the child and labeling what they are doing. For example, when a toddler is reaching for your purse, you can say, *"Oh, would you like to play with my purse? Okay, I will share with you. You asked and I let you have a turn. That is sharing."* Or, when a toddler is reaching for your peach, you can say, *"Oh, would you like a bite of my peach? Okay, I'm happy to share with you. You asked for some and I gave it to you. That is sharing."* Similarly, find times the toddler can share. Perhaps when she has a lot of mashed potatoes you can ask for a bite. If the child agrees, you can say, *"Thank you. You shared your mashed potatoes with me."* Adults can model asking and sharing between themselves as well.

Emotion coaching. Emotion coaching increases the possibility that toddlers will share. A University of Washington study reported that young children who shared more quickly and more often had parents who asked them to label feelings and to explain the emotions depicted in picture books.

Experience with young children. When toddlers have a sibling or other toddlers around who use a variety of strategies to share, toddlers can learn several ways to share. Conversely, if a toddler is in a setting where someone is always removing his toys, he may decide that he has no right to the toys and give up, or he might conclude toys go to the strongest person and put up resistance.

Family rules about toy use. Clear rules about toy possession and sharing make it easier for toddlers to learn what is acceptable. Different families have different rules. That is okay as long as the rules are consistent from day to day.

There are three approaches to who may use a toy: individual ownership, group ownership, and a blend. *With individual ownership* a toy belongs to the person to whom it was given. That child has the right to say who may use it, and when and where they may use it. When there is only one child in a family, this works fine. When several other children are involved it becomes challenging. (See "Strategies for dividing items," page 22.)

With *group ownership* all the toys belong to all the children. The question then becomes who has a right to use the toy *now?* It could be the child using it, the child who has been waiting, or perhaps the youngest child. ("Let the baby use it. When she is done, it will be your turn.")

As expected with *a blend,* families combine elements of both approaches. One way parents do that is to permit a child to have a couple of special (or precious) toys that they keep in their room when they are not using them. All other toys (those left in the common rooms) may be used by anyone. If a child leaves a special toy in the common area, it too may be used by anyone. The child must wait until the other child is done using it before returning it to his room.

It matters less what the rule is than that the rule is consistently enforced. If the rule is inconsistently enforced, kids have trouble figuring out what the rule really is.

We have looked at how toddlers understand sharing and some factors that influence how easily children learn to share. Next, we will look at five strategies for sharing and then look at how you can teach these skills.

✴ Five Sharing Strategies

Some toddlers who are observant and adapt easily pick up strategies for sharing quickly. Other toddlers need to be taught specific strategies and practice them over and over again until they feel comfortable with the new approaches before they venture to use them with others.

Five strategies toddlers can learn are to ask, take turns, trade, wait, and divide the items. When children are older you can add interactive play and cooperative play, however, these are beyond the scope of this book. We will briefly describe each strategy, discuss any challenges, and offer a "teaching script."

1. Asking

Asking is a popular adult strategy. Toddlers are often told, "*If you want something, ask for it. Don't grab it.*" As children grow, it is important for them to be able to ask for what they want. When asking another child to use the toy he or she is playing with, the asking can be verbal or nonverbal.

....

Challenge 3: *Toddler's asking for a toy rarely works.*

....

An informal study in a laboratory preschool found that "asking for a toy" worked 7% of the time. If that is the only strategy you offer toddlers you are setting them up for failure 93% of the time.

Possible solution: Teach toddlers several strategies. You might want to teach one a week or maybe one a month until they are all introduced.

Steps in asking

Children go through several stages as they learn to ask for a toy: beginner, intermediate, and experienced. We will look at how each of these might play out.

Beginner dialog — Ask for toy

Alex: [Extending his hand] *Truck?* Or, *May I have the truck?*
Jason: *No.*
Alex: [Grabs the truck or cries.]

Improvement: Asking for a *turn* is often more successful than asking to use or have the item now.

Intermediate dialog — Ask for turn

Alex: *May I have a turn with the truck?*
Jason: *No. I'm using it.*
Alex: [Cries. (He asked nicely and was refused.)]

....

Challenge 4: *Toddlers often get upset when children refuse their requests.*

....

Asking implies the person asked has the right to say "yes" or "no." Your child will probably receive far more "nos" than "yeses." It rarely helps to tell your child to "Relax. It's not the end of the world. You will get a chance to play with the toy later." First, toddlers live VERY in the present. It feels to them that if they don't have it now, they will never have it. Second, few know (or rather few believe) that they will get a chance to use it even if they ask. Third, they are only learning to manage their feelings.

Possible solution: Teach the toddler specific tools to deal with his disappointment. You can teach your toddler to take a deep breath, shake out his mads, or take a sip of water. *Note:* Teaching kids to deal with disappointment takes time and energy — however, it saves you grief in the long run and prepares them for adulthood. A process for teaching toddlers (and others) self-calming tools is on page 25.

Another step in asking. Request a turn "when you are done." This is even more likely to be successful than asking for a turn now.

Experienced dialog — Ask when you may use it

Alex: *Hi, Jason. May I have a turn with the truck?*
Jason: *No. I'm using it.*
Alex: *May I use it when you're done?*

> ### Teaching self-calming skills takes time
>
> Teaching about feelings is a lot like teaching a language — what you work on now will begin to come together in three to six months.
>
> To manage their feelings toddlers need to have a feelings vocabulary, understand about feelings (they all are okay, they change, they are different from actions, etc.), and have several self-calming strategies.
>
> You can find out more about teaching "emotional competence" in my book, *Dealing with Disappointment: Helping Kids Cope When Things Don't Go Their Way.*

Jason: *Umm. Maybe.*

Alex: *When will you be done?* [Count minutes on a timer, laps around the room or table, etc.] Jason: *Umm. Three minutes.*

Progress is being made. Alex asked and now has Jason's agreement to use the truck, but no truck yet.

Challenge 5: *Toddlers need to learn to wait for a turn.*

Many adults are tempted to distract the child until the truck is available. That makes sense as a short-term strategy, however, in the long run it teaches the child to be dependent on someone else for happiness and problem solving.

Possible solution: You guessed it, *teach* the child to wait. That is one of our five strategies. Learn about strategies for waiting on page 14.

How to teach asking

Three approaches to teaching "asking" suggest themselves.

Model sharing with other adults (partner or coworkers). Remember to include both acceptance and rejection of request. *May I use the pen? . . . Yes . . . Thank you.* Or, *May I use your pen? . . . No . . . Okay, maybe later.*

Speak for the child. Go with the child. Kneel behind him and ask the other child, *"May Alex use the truck when you are done?"* Then interpret the response, *"Oh, you're not done yet? Alex will wait until you're done."*

Practice with puppets (or trucks, or stuffed animals). Begin by playing both the asking and responding parts. Then involve the child. Kitty puppet can ask Puppy puppet for a turn with the train. You can ask your child, *"What do you think Puppy will say?"*

Asking for a toy is a socially acceptable approach to sharing, but one that rarely gets the desired item. We will now look at taking turns.

2. Taking turns

Taking turns involves *serial* "possession" of an item, —switching "ownership" back and forth. As we mentioned in the development section, toddlers are very concerned with their own needs and wishes, so they are not very good at serial possession. In the beginning, it is helpful if the turns are very, very short. As toddlers learn to trust they will get the item back, the turns can become longer.

Taking turns is a basic skill in our society. In addition to taking turns with toys we also take turns talking, working, waiting for assistance, and playing games.

How to introduce taking turns

Most people find the easiest way to begin taking turns is with a ball.

Start with short turns. Roll a ball back and forth saying, *"My turn, your turn, my turn, your turn"* as the ball changes ownership. For most toddlers rolling the ball back and forth is more fun than holding it by themselves.

Slowly lengthen the possession time before you return the ball. You can start this once the child is comfortable taking quick turns with the ball. You might bounce the ball once before returning it to the toddler. When that is comfortable, toss it in the air a couple of times. Gradually lengthen the time you take.

Next you can change the item. At first, keep the turns short and then gradually stretch them. You could:
• Roll a car (or truck) back and forth.

- Alternate holding a doll for a couple of seconds, then passing it back.
- Take turns crawling through a tunnel or sitting in a cardboard box.
- Alternate walking on a line (masking tape on the floor) or jumping over a book.
- Take turns eating raisins (cut grapes, M&Ms) from a plate. (To extend time between turns you could do "Clap, Snap, Slap" or rest your hands in your lap between "takes.")

You can even say your feet are taking turns as you go upstairs — right foot up, left foot up, right foot up, left foot up, etc. The idea is to help the toddler see that taking turns is a natural part of life.

When you introduce the concept of taking turns, who goes first is not an issue. However, when young children begin to take turns with other toddlers who want the same item, who goes first often becomes stressful.

....

Challenge 6: *Toddlers need to learn strategies to decide who goes first.*

....

For young children, *who goes first* can be a deal breaker in sharing. It is back to their belief that possession equals ownership and to their lack of self-restraint.

Possible solution: Teach them several decision-making strategies. Yes, it is the old "T" word again. The strategy could be picture pull, photo toss, coin toss, dice roll, a game ("Paper, scissor, stone" or "Engine, engine number nine . . ."), the day, even–odd calendar day. Or the youngest could always go first. These strategies are described below.

Strategies for who goes first

Picture pull. Print or cut a picture of the face of each child likely to be involved and put them in your pocket or a little bowl. When a conflict occurs, draw a picture to choose who goes first.

Picture coin toss for two. Cut out a picture of each child. Glue one to each side of the rolled metal end of a frozen orange juice can. (See illustration.) When two kids want a toy, toss the picture coin to see who gets it first.

Name sticks. Write each child's name on a popsicle stick. Put the sticks in a cup with the blank end showing. When a conflict occurs, a child draws one stick and you look to see whose name is on it.

Dice roll. Get a large die. If you have two kids, color the dots two different colors (white and black are easiest). If you have three kids, use three colors. When a conflict occurs, roll the die and see which color is up.

Coin toss. Get a large coin. Point out that one side has a head and one has something else. (Give the sides a name — building, horse, plant, etc.) Assign each child to a side (Anna is head, Brittany is house.) Toss the coin and see what comes up.

Child of the day. One child is the ruler of the day. When there is a conflict, that child makes the decision (gets what he or she wants). Mark a calendar with a symbol for each child. When there is a conflict, both (all) kids go to the calendar and see who gets it.

Games. When kids get older they can use games or chants to determine who is first. Some games are "Paper, scissor, rock," "Engine, engine number nine," or "Eeny, meeny, miney, moe." Directions are available on the Internet.

Name log. Whenever there is a conflict, children alternate who "wins." If there are three children, each will win every third time. To keep track of who was the winner last time, a paper is kept on the refrigerator or door. Each time the person invoked the privilege, their name, date, and issue are added to the list. Toddlers can use a stamp to record their "win."

To get started taking turns you could write each child's name on slips of paper and draw one. You could continue to use that strategy or rotate through the other strategies and find the one your kids like best.

We have looked at strategies for deciding who goes first. Sometime toddlers, particularly young ones, also need help knowing when their turn is over.

Strategies for ending turns

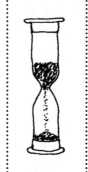

When you roll a ball back and forth or walk up stairs there is a natural rhythm that ends each turn and makes it easy to take turns. However, for using a special truck or holding a new doll there is no natural end. Children need ways to know their turn is over.

Three strategies you can use are: a timer, counting (trips), and completion (or interest wanes).

A timer may be the simplest way to end a turn. It is objective and it can be set by either an adult or a child. A timer with a long ring usually works better than one with a single ding. A children's or plastic hourglass can work also.

Counting has the advantage of always being available. You can count the number of trips around the room a child drives. One trip is often a good place to start with young toddlers and then trade. Or you could link to the child's age. One trip for a one-year-old. Two trips for a two-year-old. Decide in advance what the number will be. *"You may hang two tree ornaments, then it's Adrian's turn,"* or *"You may plant one flower and then it is Noah's turn."*

Completion. Another approach is to let a child play with something until he or she is done. Proponents of this approach believe it helps children experience "enough" and over time to share more willingly. To do this you need to clarify what "done" means. Usually it means when a child puts the item down and moves away from it. Some child care centers and preschools that use this approach keep a list of children waiting for the toy or turn.

Taking turns is part of our social culture; however, it is very difficult for toddlers to take turns until they know how to wait.

3. Waiting

The ability to wait pleasantly is a wonderful life skill — useful for both children and adults. We often tell children to wait and expect them to do it — as though waiting were as natural as breathing. For some children it may come naturally and for many others it must be taught.

There are three steps in waiting. First, to calm yourself down if upset. Second, to figure out how to wait (what to do with the time), and third, how to recognize the end. Teaching self-calming is discussed briefly in the section on "Teaching Coping Strategies" on page 23, so we will move on to waiting strategies.

Strategies for waiting

There are many strategies for waiting. Most people have strategies they use, but they may not be aware of them — much less be able to teach the waiting strategies to their toddler. Let's first look at strategies for young toddlers and then look at ones suitable for older toddlers and kids.

YOUNGER TODDLERS

Do something else — Find a book, puzzle, similar toy, or run in place. Initially, you will need to interest the child in a toy or activity. Some people call this distraction, which in fact it is. However, if you take it one step further and teach the child how to find something, then it becomes a coping strategy. We will talk more about this in the section on how to teach waiting (page 17).

Sing a song — Again you will probably need to sing the song for (or with) the toddler until they are comfortable with the song. Use songs that are familiar to toddlers. If the song has hand motions that usually helps. Several songs that work for many kids are "Eensy Weensy Spider," "Wheels on the Bus," "If You're Happy and You Know It," etc.

In the beginning you can simply sing the song. Then you can ask, *"Would you like to sing the spider song or the wheels on the bus song?"* After he is comfortable choosing you can ask, *"What song would you like to sing?"* so he gets experience of *thinking* of the songs while he waits.

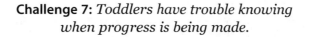

Challenge 7: *Toddlers have trouble knowing when progress is being made.*

We often tell children to wait. We repeatedly verbalize the need for children to delay their wishes. Rarely do parents say *"I'm half done,"* or *"I am done _____ now. It is time to stop waiting."* Without the verbal closure, toddlers often feel waiting is endless.
Possible solution: Teach toddlers to notice progress of time.

Notice progress. One reason waiting is so hard for children is that they don't see progress. You can teach kids to look for progress clues. One way to illustrate *physical change* is at a park or beach. You can watch the tide come in or a tree shadow lengthen. If you put a stick in the ground at the edge of the water or shadow, you can see the movement.

You can also notice progress by *narrating the change.* Describe it as a sportscaster might. If your child is waiting for a scooter another child has agreed to give up after a ride around the room you could say, *"Aiden has a good start, he's halfway to the wall, now is he rounding the corner and going behind the sofa. . . . Ah, here he comes out from behind the sofa. He is passing the kitchen door. He is halfway around the track. Now he is . . ."* With the narration you are not only entertaining the child during the wait, but showing the child how to notice progress.

Daily routine units. Another way to judge the passage of time is with "daily routine units." These are common events in the toddler's life that generally take the same length of time. For example, singing "Twinkle, Twinkle Little Star," a trip to check the mail box, a kid's video, a bath, or the time at pre-school. You could tell the toddler, *"It will be your turn in the length of the twinkle song."*

When children have more language skill and experience in the world, there are more waiting activities you can introduce.

Categories. Point out (or count) something: people, cars, circles, squares, tiles on floor, buildings. For young toddlers this could be adapted so the child points to them as the adult counts.

Play a looking (observation) game. "I Spy Something Red," "Big & Little," or "Alphabet Hunt."

Make up stories. Say, *"What would you do if . . . ,"* or *"What is Tomás* [or any story character] *doing now?"* or play back-and-forth, where each person takes turns telling a couple of sentences.

Talk to someone (real or imaginary). If there is a friend or a parent to talk with, fine. If not, pretend to talk to Daddy or Grandma or a favorite auntie. You could introduce this with, *"I have a magic phone* [old phone, throat lozenge box, or simple finger phone]. *Who would you like to talk to?"*

Do something physical. Shake the sillies out, swing around a lamp or signpost, skip, jump in place or over a stone or book.

When you go out (to the park or a playdate) you can bring something fun to use if your child needs to wait — a small book, chalk, deck of cards, small cars, dolls, or plastic animals.

Determining the end of waiting

Hopefully, when a toddler starts to wait there is a defined end to the waiting. It can be a length of time (two minutes), a task completed (all the pieces are in the puzzle), or a specific number of "rounds" or "tries" (ride the scooter around the room once). These are the same as the strategies for ending turns we looked at in the previous section ("Taking turns").

How to teach waiting

To teach the concept of waiting you need to introduce the concept, demonstrate how to wait, and practice using the technique. Teaching the concept is sandwiched in between helping the child calm himself down if upset and learning to recognize the end of waiting. You can teach the strategy of waiting by modeling it, demonstrating the process, and practicing it over and over.

Model and comment. The easiest way to introduce waiting is by modeling it. If no situation comes naturally, you can stage one with your partner or a friend.

For example, when your spouse is on the computer, you could ask, *"May I use the computer?"* If he says *"No,"* you could say, *"When may I have a turn?"* or, *"When will you be done?"* When he says, *"Ten minutes,"* you can say, *"Okay."* Then reflect, *"First, I will set a timer to tell me to check back. Then, what can I do for 10 minutes? Let me see, I could look at a book or wash the dishes. Which will I try first? I'll wash the dishes because that will take about 10 minutes."* When the timer rings, you can say, *"Oh good, it is time to check if Daddy is done with the computer."*

You can also model waiting for a cake to finish baking or Daddy to get home from work (if you know he is on the way).

Demonstrate a couple of activities. You can offer a similar item, a near item, or one far away. Each approach has pros and cons. A *similar item* might satisfy the need or it might emphasize the loss. A *near item* is quick but may not engage the toddler's interest. A *far away item* may decrease the call of the wanted item or increase the tension by increasing the distance.

For example, suppose you have just helped Ethan ask to use the truck Daniel has. Daniel said, "No," and Ethan has to wait for a turn.

Mom: *Daniel is still using the truck. What can you do while you wait?*
Ethan: [No answer]
Mom: *Let's see what is near that might be interesting. Would you like this truck?*

Ethan: [Shakes his head no.]

Mom: *What about this truck? It's an aid car. Vroom, vroom."*

Ethan: [Shakes his head again.]

Mom: *Looks like you don't want a different truck. Let's sit over there and read a story while we wait.*

Ethan: [Nods sadly.]

Note: When Ethan gets a turn, comment, *"Daniel's done. Now you're finished waiting."*

Practice waiting skills. Probably the two most effective things you can do to help toddlers wait are to comment on progress and to help them learn to occupy themselves. For example, if you were going to change your clothes you could tell your child, *"I'm going to change my clothes. You can play with the trucks or look at a book while you wait for me."*

Or, if you were kneading bread and your daughter wants you to pick her up, you could say, *"Mommy will pick you up as soon as my hands are clean. Wait while I wash my hands. I am turning the water on and putting soap on my hands. Now I am rubbing them together. I have lots of bubbles so now I'm rinsing my hands, next I will dry them. Thank you for waiting. Now my hands are clean and dry. I can pick you up."*

Waiting is a very useful strategy; however, it does involve delayed gratification. A strategy that may yield the toys sooner is trading.

4. Trading

Trading is pretty simple from an adult point of view. One child offers another child a similar or more interesting toy, hoping to get a desired toy in return. The difficulty for young toddlers is switching focus from wanting the toy NOW to figuring out what the other child might like. In the beginning, you will need to model (and verbalize) the process of trading and of selecting a toy to trade. The easiest way to teach this is in four small steps.

Use small steps to teach trading

The goal of small steps is to gradually shift the selection and offering of a toy from the adult to the toddler. Let's call the child who is using the toy, the "possessor," and the child who wants the toy, the "toddler."

Model trading a toy and describing the process. When you demonstrate the process, comment or reflect on what the possessor usually likes — trucks, dinosaurs, books, baby dolls, etc. Make a point of looking around to see what might appeal to the possessor. Select a toy, stating why it might appeal to the other child. Offer the possessor the alternate toy and wait for a response. Continue to offer desirable toys until a compelling toy is found or you decide to change approach.

Give the toddler a toy to trade. Select a toy you are pretty sure is attractive to the possessor. Give it to the toddler and ask her to trade. The toddler may need to wait for a response or you may need to interpret the possessor's response.

Offer the toddler two or three toys and ask her to choose one to trade. She needs to begin to think what the other child would like.

Ask the toddler to find a toy to trade. Initially, you may need to offer suggestions about what types of toys the possessor may like or even suggest a couple of specific toys.

....

Challenge 8: *Toddlers have trouble figuring out what other children might like.*

....

Figuring out what other people would like is hard for toddlers. Children do not learn to take the perspective of another person until early to middle elementary school. However, many young children can *remember* what items other kids have used and therefore might like.

Possible solution: You can help toddlers observe what other kids like, recall what they used previously, and experiment with what they might like to try.

A successful horse-trading story

Sixteen-month-old Joey wanted the rocking horse that Nicholas, almost two, was using. Joey's language was minimal so he pointed to the horse and said, "Unh, unh, unh," meaning "I want to use the rocking horse." Nicholas ignored him and continued to rock leisurely back and forth.

After a bit, Joey stopped whimpering and went to get a noise-making pull toy. He dragged the intriguing toy around the front of the rocking horse through Nicholas's field of vision. Nicholas stopped and stared, hopped off the horse, and ran to the pull toy. Joey abandoned the pull toy and climbed onto the rocking horse. Joey got what he wanted by trading a pull toy for the rocking horse. The trade took place so quietly that if the teacher had not been watching how kids use the rocking horse, she would never have noticed!

Teaching scripts for trading

Below are three scripts in which the parent gradually turns responsibility for the selection and offering of an alternate item over to the child.

1. Adult models and narrates the process of trading.
Peter is trying to grab an elephant from Ethan.

Mom [to Peter]: *Peter, let's see if Ethan will trade something for the elephant. I wonder what Ethan might like? Hmm. He played with the giraffe yesterday. I wonder if he would like it today?*
Mom: [to Ethan as she holds the giraffe up and tilts it back and forth] *Ethan, would you like to trade animals?*
Ethan: [Reaches towards the giraffe.]
Mom: [Holds her hand out near the elephant to receive it.] *Would you like to trade?*
Ethan: [Drops the elephant into Mom's hand and takes the giraffe.]
Mom: [To Ethan] *Thank you for trading.* [To Peter] *Ethan traded animals. Now it is your turn with the elephant.*

2. Toddler chooses which of two items Mom will offer.

Mom: *Let's see if Ethan will trade. Do you think he would prefer the lion or the giraffe?* [Mom holds both toys out for Peter to choose one.]

Peter: [Points to the lion.]

Mom: *You think Ethan would like the lion? Let's try and see.*

Mom: [To Ethan, offering the lion] *Ethan, would you like to trade animals?*

Ethan: [Turns away from the lion and pulls the elephant closer.]

Mom: *Looks like you don't want to trade the elephant now. Let's see if we can find something else.*

When Peter can comfortably choose between two items, you can offer him three or more items to choose among.

3. Child chooses and offers a toy.

Mom: *Peter, it looks like you want the elephant that Ethan has. You can find something he might like and offer to trade. Let's walk over to the toy shelf and you can choose something for him.*

Peter: [Selects a truck to offer and looks apprehensive.]

Mom: *Would you like me to go with you?* [Peter nods. Mom goes with Peter and stands behind him.]

Peter offers the alternative. Ethan lets go of the elephant and Peter takes it.

Mom: *Peter, you offered Ethan a truck and he traded.*

The ability to trade depends more on experience than on language or age. Some children catch on very easily (as Joey in the horse-trading story). Others take many repetitions to learn the concept. The next, and last, strategy for sharing we will look at is dividing the items.

5. Dividing the items

Dividing items is hard for many toddlers because they see it as "ownership" lost rather than "use" gained. In the beginning, the grown-up will need to divide the items for children. Toddlers judge volume visually rather than by number of items. So, when you divide things, make the piles visually equal rather than quantitatively equal. As with the other strategies, if you verbalize the process, it will help the toddler understand.

For example, you could say, *"Hmm, we have two boys and they both want to play with the Duplos. What can we do so they can both be happy? I know, we can split the blocks into two piles. Each boy can have some."* If one of the little guys cries that he wants more, you can introduce the concept of "enough." *"You'd like more blocks. Noah is using those blocks. You have enough Duplos."*

Strategies for dividing items

When toddlers get comfortable with having toys divided, you can begin to talk about different ways to split things.

Characteristics of items. You can divide things several ways. For example, you could split vehicles by size, purpose (e.g., trucks vs. cars), or simply random. You could divide blocks by color, size, shape, or random.

Many things can be divided: cars and trucks, blocks, dolls and doll clothes, books, dinosaurs, crayons, play dough, and sand toys. When adults divide items it tends to be random. However, when kids are dividing the toys between them, both (or all) children usually want to participate.

There are two common strategies for kids dividing things — taking turns picking; and one child divides, the other chooses.

Take turns dividing. Once toddlers can take turns rolling a ball back and forth or alternating taking raisins off a plate, you can begin to help them take turns dividing toys. In the beginning, an adult may need to verbalize turn taking: *"Jacob's turn. Noah's turn. Jacob's turn. Noah's turn."* Once they get in the rhythm you can stop directing until needed again.

One child divides, the other chooses. This approach is beyond most toddlers but so helpful I wish to introduce it. With this strategy one child divides the item or items and the second child chooses which part they want. For example, if two children wanted the same banana they could each have a part. One child could cut the banana in half and the second child would choose which half he or she wanted. The beauty of this approach is that it is in the first child's best interest to make the division as fair as possible because she will get what is left.

We have looked at five strategies for sharing: asking, taking turns, waiting, trading, and dividing the toys. Eventually, children learn that they can own something while someone else uses it. In the meantime, you can teach specific skills kids can use. In the next section, we will look at how to teach social skills, then we will look at dealing with common challenges.

✳ Teaching Coping Strategies

Teaching social skills, like sharing and managing your feelings, involves more than telling children what to do. Generally, it takes between 50 and 1,000 repetitions for a child to learn a desired skill.

How to teach a sharing strategy

Suppose your child has to practice waiting 500 times before she "gets it." You can step back and wait while she experiments and hope she chooses an acceptable strategy; or you can set up situations to offer information and encourage desired strategies. The steps to teach a coping strategy are present, practice, and prompt.

Present the concept. It doesn't matter how clear sharing, asking, or waiting are to you. If the child doesn't understand or feel comfortable with it, the strategy will not succeed. Temperament plays a part here — toddlers who resist new things will take longer to learn specific strategies simply because they are new.

You can present the strategy by modeling, noticing others using the strategy and labeling what they do, or setting up a teaching scenario. Many of the sharing strategies below have scripts or ideas for introducing the approach.

Practice, practice, practice. Practicing a strategy may not make sharing perfect, but it dramatically increases the odds the tools will be used. Use puppets, stories, board games, trains, and conversation to practice new skills. Practicing in pretend will shorten the number of times kids will need to experiment in real life before learning the strategy.

To practice, you can use puppets, stuffed animals, trucks, books, or role plays. For example, Kitty puppet can ask Puppy puppet for a turn with the truck. You can ask your child, *"What do you think Puppy will say?"* Then you can switch the puppet roles and say, *"Puppy wants the book that Kitty is looking at. What can Puppy do?"*

When you practice keep the tone light, fun, and curious. Practice is not a test. It is helpful to stop while the activity is still fun. Many short sessions generally work better than fewer long sessions. How long this step takes depends on your child's adaptability and her response to new things. If she is slow to adapt and dislikes new things in general, it will take much longer.

When to change your expectation

When your child has demonstrated the ability to use a strategy in pretend, then you can prompt him or her to use the strategy in real life. If toddlers cannot use a strategy in pretend, then it is unreasonable to expect them to do it under the stress of real life.

Prompt in real life. When your child has demonstrated the ability to use a strategy in pretend, then you can prompt him or her to use the strategy in real life. If toddlers cannot use a strategy in pretend, then it is unreasonable to expect them to do it under the stress of real life.

In the beginning you may want to suggest a specific tool, *"Looks like you want to use the truck. You can ask Brian if you may have a turn with the truck."* When Brian says, *"No,"* you can say, *"Brian is not done yet. What can you do to wait until he is done with his turn?"*

When your child gets comfortable using specific tools in real life you can *offer him a choice.* For example, *"Looks like you want to use the truck. Do you want to ask or to trade?"*

When your child can easily decide between two or three choices, you can *ask him to think of ideas* himself. For example, *"You'd like to play with that puzzle. What can you do?"* Once your child can think of strategies it is time to turn the whole task over to him or her.

This process of gradually turning responsibility over to the child (suggest a strategy, offer a choice, ask for an idea) can be used for encouraging most desirable behavior. You can read more about the approach in my book, *Am I Doing Too Much for My Child?*

It is easier for children to make good decisions when they are calm. In the next section we will look briefly at how to teach a self-calming tool.

How to teach a self-calming tool

One of the tasks in toddlerhood is learning to manage feelings. Until they do, when toddlers can't have something NOW they have a tantrum.

....

Challenge 9: *Toddlers are just beginning to learn self-calming skills.*

....

Many parents and caregivers try to teach self-calming tools while the child is having a tantrum. This rarely works.

Possible solution: Teach specific self-soothing strategies when the child is calm. During an emotional outburst is not a "teachable moment."

There are many strategies children can use to calm themselves. The most common ones for toddlers are sucking (a pacifier or liquid through a straw), taking a deep breath, shaking out the feelings, and getting a hug. These tools and many more are presented in my book, *Dealing with Disappointment: Helping Kids Cope When Things Don't Go Their Way.*

Teaching children to calm themselves involves more than saying, "When you are upset, take a deep breath."

Introduce the activity. The child needs to feel comfortable with the activity before he can use the activity to calm himself. Adam loves to sit under a tree in the shade, so his dad teaches him to save the calmness he feels in his mind and go there when he is upset. Dad begins by sitting with Adam under a tree in the shade and talking about how the sunlight filters through the leaves, the sounds that he hears, and the way the breeze feels on his skin.

Link tool to feeling calm. Dad says to Adam, *"My, how pleasant it feels to sit here. I feel calm all over. I'm going to soak up this calmness so I can use it when I need it."* Or, sometime when things are going well, he might say, *"Adam, let's sit here and go to the calm place."* His purpose is to associate the action with a feeling of calmness and well-being.

Practice using the tool. When Adam can associate calmness with the technique, he practices using the tool in pretend. Dad says, *"Adam, remember this morning when Brian was mean and you started crying? I'm going to pretend Brian is being mean to me, and I'll try to stay calm by going to the calm place in my mind."* After he models the tool, he invites Adam to practice going to the calm place in his mind.

Parents can help kids practice using the calming technique in three ways:

• *Act out a situation* with the child watching. The child can practice using the technique to respond to the situation.

• *Rehearse in pretend.* Make up a story and act it out. Parent can invite the child to use the techniques learned.

• *Replay real (recognizable)* situation. If the child has had a problem, a parent can set the stage and the child can practice using the strategy.

The more times you practice in pretend successfully, the fewer times you will need to practice in real life.

Prompt the child to use the tool. Once Adam can use a tool in pretend, Dad prompts him when he is upset. *"Would you like to take deep breaths or go to a calm place in your mind?"* It helps to offer the choice before the child has totally lost control.

Back out and let a child cope. When your child can choose to calm himself or herself when prompted, it is time to back out and let your child remember without prompting.

Although parents are often motivated to teach when kids are upset, that is not usually a good time for children to learn. Once your child can use a calming tool in pretend, you can suggest it when they are upset.

Next, we will look at several common situations where sharing, or lack of it, becomes difficult.

✳ Common Situations

To learn to share, kids need strategies and practice with other children. Once kids start playing with (or near) other children several frustrating situations arise. You may find your child grabbing rather than using the skills you have practiced, or she may not want to share her toys at home even though she can usually take turns when she is elsewhere.

Below are several common situations, with strategies other parents have used successfully.

··

Challenge 10: *Toddlers often grab toys they want from other children.*

··

Toddlers believe the only time is NOW. If they don't have it, they will never have it, so grabbing seems reasonable to them.

Possible solution: Establish clear (predictable) rules of use, teach alternate strategies for getting what you want, and comment on their success when they get the item they want in an acceptable way (waiting, trading, etc.). This process will take time.

What to do when kids grab

Sometimes parents or caregivers are tempted to scold or punish toddlers when they try to grab a toy. Understandable as that is, it rarely helps. Usually it works better to treat grabbing as a teachable moment. The following scripts support the approach that whoever has the toy first may continue using it until they are done. I first learned these scripts from Karen Truelove, an experienced preschool teacher.

We will look at grabbing in three situations:
- one child clearly had it first
- one child had it first but doesn't care
- it is unclear who had it first

Megan clearly has the truck, and Amy wants it.

- **Adult clarifies the situation for each child and observes.**

Adult to Megan: *"Hold on tight, Megan! You can tell Amy, 'STOP! My turn'."*

Adult to Amy: *"Look! Megan's hands are on the truck. She is holding on tight. She is still having a turn with the truck. When her turn is done, you can have a turn. I can help you wait. We can play until it's your turn, if you want."*

- **Adult pauses and observes.**
- **If Amy lets go** of the item, the adult acknowledges the child's effort. *"Wow! You let go fast. Thanks for letting go."* [This is the end of this thread.]
- **If Amy continues** to hold on or pulls the item away, the adult coaches her.

Adult says, *"You need to let go of the truck. It's still Megan's turn."*

- **Adult pauses and observes.**

1. If the child lets go by herself, acknowledge her effort. Say, *"Thank you for letting go, Amy. You did it all by yourself. Let's see what we can do while you wait for your turn. I like to play with you."*

2. If the child continues to hold, offer her a choice, *"Amy, you can let go of the truck by yourself or I can help you let go this time."*

- **Adult pauses and observes.**

3. If the child doesn't let go by herself, follow through with the choice. Gently remove her hands from the item while saying, *"I know it's sad to let go. You really want a turn with the truck. I will wait with you for your turn."*

❷
Megan lets go of the item and doesn't seem to care that it has been taken away.

- **Adult clarifies the situation.**

  Adult to the first child, *"Megan, you can tell Amy, 'STOP! My turn,' if you still want a turn with the truck."*

- **Adult pauses and observes.**

- **If Megan indicates** by words or body language that she still wants her turn, then assist her through the process above and make sure she gets to continue her turn with the item.

- **If Megan does not seem to care** about the item, she may not want it, but at least she hears and knows that she could still have a turn if she wanted. She does not have to be a "victim."

❸
Two children have hold of the item, and the adult does not know which one of the children had it first.

- **Adult clarifies the situation and observes.**

  Adult to children: *"Whoa! Two people want the truck. We have a problem to figure out. I wish that I had more trucks so that everyone could have one at the same time. I only have one truck. Somebody needs to let go."*

- **Adult pauses and observes.**

  Hopefully, one person will let go.

- **Adult offers structure if neither child lets go.**

  1. If neither lets go, say, *"What should we do? Amy and Megan both want a turn with the truck. I don't know who had it first."*

  2. If one of them lets go, say, *"Thanks for letting go. I'll make sure that you get a turn soon. We can play together while you wait, if you want to."*

  3. If both are still holding on, you can say *"We can draw names out of my pocket (or special bag, box, or bowl) to see who goes now."*

Sharing at home

Most toddlers find it more difficult to share toys in their own home than elsewhere. Here are some strategies that may help.

Let the child put some "special" toys away. It can be a specific number of toys like two or three that she doesn't have to share with others, or it can be a volume of toys. Put the toys she doesn't want to share on her bedroom shelf or in her crib. Putting special toys away often helps.

Rehearse appropriate actions when remaining toys are used. This is the practice, practice, practice part of teaching mentioned previously. Once another child shows interest in a toy, that toy becomes "special," even if it has not been touched in a month.

You can make a story (or puppet play) to illustrate what will happen if she wants the toy the guest has. See *Kitty's playdate story* in the sidebar for an example.

Clarify family rules. Family rules might be: (1) Put toys you don't want to share on your bed. (2) All remaining toys may be used by anyone. (3) If you want something someone else is using ask, trade, or wait for a turn. (4) Let the guest have the first turn with a toy because he or she doesn't have a chance to play with that toy very often.

Start with a neutral activity. Something like dancing to music, play dough, or coloring that the kids can do together. In the summer they could run through a sprinkler or splash in a wading pool. When it is raining they can splash in water puddles. In the snow they can make tracks or piles of snow.

Remind your child that the toy belongs to him even when the guest uses it. Tell him, *"Your car will stay here when Ian leaves. I will not let Ian take the toy home."* Then, when the guest has left, point out that the toy is still here and thank him for letting the guest use it. The next time the guest comes you can remind him, *"Remember last time Ian was here? You let him hold the car while he was here. And Ian left the car here when he went home."*

Kitty's playdate story

Kitty's friend Puppy was coming over. Kitty collected her favorite things: her teddy bear, a stuffed mouse, and *Goodnight Moon* book. She put them on her bed and covered them with a blanket.

Mama Cat reminded Kitty that she needed to let Puppy use the other toys if he wanted.

Ring. Puppy was at the door. Mama Cat opened the door and Puppy came in. He wandered around a bit until he saw the blue ball. He likes balls so he picked it up. Immediately Kitty said, "No. Mine."

Mama Cat reminded Kitty that it was her ball, and she could let Puppy have a turn. It would still be her ball. Mama Cat asked Kitty if she would like to find a toy to trade or wait until Puppy was done.

Kitty decided to trade. She found a feather bird and offered it to Puppy. But Puppy didn't like it. Kitty thought some more and got her noisy-ball. She rolled it by Puppy. Puppy stopped playing with the blue ball and picked up the noisy-ball.

Mama Cat said, "Kitty, you traded for the blue ball. First you offered the feather bird and Puppy said, 'No.' Then you offered the noisy-ball and Puppy liked that."

Keep initial playdates short. Many young children find it stressful to share their things, even when they have been told that the other child(ren) will not take them home. When people are stressed, it is more difficult to make good decisions. Ideally, the guest would leave before the kids have a meltdown. Plan for an hour and extend it if things go well. If that is too long, you can plan a shorter time, or wait a month or two.

Sharing on a playdate

Many toddlers will not be willing or able to share their own toys, but may have little problem sharing other people's toys. Several things you can do to increase the odds that things go well are:

• Schedule the playdate when your toddler is rested and fed.
• Rehearse/practice sharing strategies (ask, trade, wait, etc.).
• Bring a toy or two your child can use if the other child is having difficulty sharing, or one he can use to trade with.
• Leave toys your child is unwilling to share at home or in the car.

Sharing at a public place

Sharing toys in public places can be difficult because there are no standard rules for how to resolve conflicts. Some people bring their own toys and monitor the children's play. Other people believe in survival of the fittest (or loudest), and let kids work things out themselves. Still others look on uncomfortably and don't know what to do.

....

Challenge 11: *Toddlers have trouble understanding that different families have different rules.*

....

When conflict arises in a public space, many people suffer in silence, not wanting to make a fuss. It is helpful to know that sometimes everyone is uncomfortable but no one wants to take the lead in responding. Sometimes, older toddlers and preschoolers find it confusing when their parent does not let them grab toys, but doesn't stop another child from grabbing a toy from them.

Possible solution: Be proactive and assertive. To be *proactive,* clarify what your expectations (family rules) are and explain that different families have different rules. You might add that you don't interfere with other family rules except in matters of safety. If sharing the playground equipment becomes a big issue, then you can distract your toddler or choose to leave.

Being *assertive* might mean alerting the other parents to what is happening or saying, *"Trouble is brewing. Do you want to handle it or do you want me to?"* Many parents will be happy for you to handle the situation because they don't want to deal with it. In the cases where they are willing to intervene but their attention had wandered, they are now aware of what is going on.

Child always lets others take things

Some toddlers let other kids take toys from them. Although it makes play harmonious, many parents are worried that their child is not being assertive or will grow up to be a victim. What can an adult do?

First, observe the child carefully. Does the yielding child seem upset? Does he or she go back to the toy when it is free? Does it happen with several children or only one? Does it happen with both older and younger children? Is the behavior new or has she always been yielding?

Think about what you notice. Some children are born generous and do not mind yielding a toy to another. As long as the toddler knows she has a right to continue using the toy, it is fine for her to yield.

Choose a response. Below are several options you have.

- Accept the child's decision. One way to create a victim is to continually protect her from experiencing the results of her decisions. If the yielder regrets loss of the toy after it is gone, you can say, *"You wish you still had the doll. Next time you can make a different choice about sharing it."*

- Set clear rules about transfer. If the rule is "You can play with a toy until you're done," then you can check that the yielder is done. You can use the scripts on page 28 and 29 in the section on "What to do when kids grab."

- Monitor the play. If the yielding happens with a specific child or older children, you might watch and identify why if you can. You may need to assure the yielder that you will help her work things out with the other child or children.

- Help the grabber wait for the yielder to respond. Sometimes a child may ask for a toy but not wait for an answer. In those cases you need to help the potential grabber to wait for the other child to answer. Again, the scripts on page 28 and 29 may help.

- Notice what you model. Do you take things from your toddler abruptly? He may conclude that older (or bigger) people can take things from smaller ones. Similarly, not letting him finish playing may lead him to conclude the best policy is to yield.

We have looked at several common situations. Now it is time to put all you have learned together.

✳ Putting It All Together

We have examined the meaning of sharing, factors affecting sharing, and five specific strategies you can teach to encourage sharing. You have read some ideas for responding to common frustrating situations. How can you put these together?

Teach specific skills

Your next step is to deliberately introduce strategies to your children. You can do this formally or casually. With a *formal approach* you could focus on one strategy a week or a month. Plan specific times to model the strategy with your partner, make puppet plays, practice with trucks or dolls, and find ways to use the strategy with your child.

With the informal approach you can incorporate encouraging sharing in your daily routine. To start, decide which strategy you would like to work on and a couple of ways you could introduce it. Post the strategy and ideas on your refrigerator or somewhere you can see them occasionally. Then as you go through your day, ask yourself, "Can I promote a sharing concept strategy while I am doing this (eating, going for a walk, reading a story, getting the toddler dressed, etc.)?"

Encourage desired behavior

When you have introduced the sharing skills several times, change will begin — probably slowly, but change nonetheless. You can help your child to use the sharing tools by acknowledging his or her effort and successes.

At first, you may hear the toddler say "Toy" or "Unh, unh," pointing to a toy to request a turn, and then grab the item when he doesn't get it promptly. Rather than feel discouraged, you can focus on the progress. Now he is at least *thinking* about asking sometimes. For example, you might say in a pleasant voice, *"I noticed you asked Adrian for the truck."* Commenting on effort has two benefits: first, it gives language to the strategy and, second, it lets your child know that trading is an acceptable behavior. You can go on to add, *"That was sharing"* or *"You were a kind friend."*

Once your child uses one strategy, it is helpful to expand the options she considers. You can do that with puppet stories where you introduce the whole process. In these interactive puppet stories (where you invite your child to participate) you practice strategies your child can try when he or she is unsuccessful on the first try.

When kids are successful comment on that too. *"You offered to trade Noah your fire engine for the aid car he was using. He agreed. Trading worked this time."* Or, *"You wanted a turn with the baby doll that Jenny was using. You offered her a turn with your new doll and she agreed. Trading worked this time."* We often tell kids what to do, and forget to notice when they do it.

The journey

As we have seen, the secret of toddler sharing is — *toddlers don't share.* They don't have the concept, skills, or necessary delayed gratification. However, there is much you can do to promote the skills toddlers need in order to share.

Teaching sharing strategies is a journey. With some toddlers the journey is bumpy, with others it is smooth. In either case, teach needed skills and encourage the seeds of sharing when you see them.

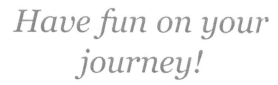

Have fun on your journey!

✳ Resources

Parenting Press has many fine books for teaching social skills. Below are books particularly helpful for teaching sharing.

Am I Doing Too Much for My Child? by Elizabeth Crary, M.S.

Children's Problem Solving series, especially *I Want It* and *I Can't Wait* by Elizabeth Crary, M.S.

Dealing with Disappointment: Helping Kids Cope When Things Don't Go Their Way by Elizabeth Crary, M.S.

Is This a Phase? Child Development & Parent Strategies, Birth to 6 Years by Helen F. Neville, B.S., R.N.

Self-Calming Cards by Elizabeth Crary, M.S., and Mits Katayama

Temperament Tools: Working with Your Child's Inborn Traits by Helen F. Neville, B.S., R.N., and Diane Clark Johnson, CFLE

Feelings for Little Children board book series: *When You're Mad and You Know it, When You're Happy . . . , When You're Shy . . . , and When You're Silly . . .* by Elizabeth Crary, M.S., and Shari Steelsmith

The Way I Feel by Janan Cain. Children can recognize their feelings from the illustrations even if they do not have the language to express them.

Two websites you might find helpful are:

- Parenting Press, http://www.parentingpress.com
- STAR Parenting, http://www.starparent.com